How to Survive Redundancy & Live the Life you want

Tony Bailey

Order this book online at www.trafford.com/09-0437
or email orders@trafford.com

Most Trafford titles are also available at major online book retailers.

Note for Librarians: A cataloguing record for this book is available from Library
and Archives Canada at www.collectionscanada.ca/amicus/index-e.html

Printed in Victoria, BC, Canada.

ISBN: 978-1-4251-0923-8 (soft)
ISBN: 978-1-4269-0925-2 (ebook)

*We at Trafford believe that it is the responsibility of us all, as both individuals
and corporations, to make choices that are environmentally and socially sound.
You, in turn, are supporting this responsible conduct each time you purchase a
Trafford book, or make use of our publishing services. To find out how you are
helping, please visit www.trafford.com/responsiblepublishing.html*

*Our mission is to efficiently provide the world's finest, most comprehensive
book publishing service, enabling every author to experience success.
To find out how to publish your book, your way, and have it available
worldwide, visit us online at www.trafford.com/10510*

 www.trafford.com

North America & international
toll-free: 1 888 232 4444 (USA & Canada)
phone: 250 383 6864 ♦ fax: 250 383 6804 ♦ email: info@trafford.com

The United Kingdom & Europe
phone: +44 (0)1865 487 395 ♦ local rate: 0845 230 9601
facsimile: +44 (0)1865 481 507 ♦ email: info.uk@trafford.com

10 9 8 7 6 5 4 3 2 1

Forward

"Life proceeds out of the intentions you have for it"

This is a self help guide intended to take you step by step through the transition from redundancy to a new life.

The guide is experiential – you own it.
It is for YOUR benefit.

The guide is here to support you.
It isn't set in stone – rather it is intended to be a catalyst in helping you to adapt to meet your changing needs and the requirements of the market.

By following the "7 steps to a new life" you can design and enjoy a richer, fuller life.

So, let's begin your journey.

Contents

CHAPTER 1

"Change is Constant" – Benjamin Disraeli

There's only one thing certain in life and that's change.

Change is natural, in many ways we're used to it. What we sometimes find hard to cope with though is the speed of change, sudden change and change which is imposed upon us - change over which we appear to have no control.

You can embrace change, making it work for you and allowing you to move on, or you can try to resist and let circumstances decide your fate.

Faced with Redundancy, you can expect to pass through several stages of your journey to a new life. These stages typically include shock, denial, frustration, acceptance, testing, integrating and assimilation.

Shock

The initial reaction to redundancy may be immobilisation, shock or sense of being overwhelmed. "What is happening to me?" "No! Not me, this can't be happening." "You can't be serious" "What have I got myself into". "Oh No!"

Denial

We often deny that change is happening by blocking out the new reality in some way. Denial results in minimising and/or externalising the change as we see it, and gives false hope - "it's nothing new after all." "It doesn't really affect me." "If I act the same way as before ....." "I don't have to do anything different." "It's all a big mistake" "I must be dreaming"

Frustration, Anger, Bargaining & Depression

As the implications of the change dawn on us, there is a turbulent period of emotion that starts with anger and hurt. This may be projected onto others or turned inwards as self-blame - "Why me, why not someone else". "I don't deserve this!" "It's their fault......" "I should have..........." "They should have ......"

This stage may be punctuated by attempts to postpone the inevitable - "Well I don't have to do anything about it right now." "If I keep my head down ......" "It will all blow over"

When the new situation can no longer be denied, pushed away or postponed, there are often feelings of uncertainty, anxiety, loss and confusion.

Acknowledgement of the necessity for change can lead to depression and a feeling of incompetence - "Will I ever be able to cope" "I can't do it, I don't have the skills". "I'm no good at this." "I'm too old, who will want to take me on"

Acceptance/Letting Go

The start of acceptance is when we are prepared to face reality and are willing to let go of the past. There's a true recognition that "the old way" is not for us anymore, and acceptance of the new circumstances. At this stage we embrace the need for change and commit to meaningful goals - "This is real", "There's no going back". "I want to be part of this," "I'm on my way".

Testing

As acceptance grows we start to experiment and try out new behaviours, testing their appropriateness to the new situation. Holding back from the "new way" is replaced by open recognition of possibilities - "What's possible here?" "Let's try it and see." "Will it work?" "Does it fit?" There is often a degree of frustration at this stage, but now it is directed at blockages in achieving the goal, rather than about being moved away from emotional investment in the past.

Integration

At this stage new strategies are proving successful. Integration is the conscious process of reflection, searching for meaning, tying together at a cognitive level what has been happening and celebrating success. "Do I understand?" "It will be OK" "This all makes sense now" "I've got it - it feels great!" "I'm on my way"

Assimilation

Beyond integration is assimilation. The change is internalised, it's part of you. It's how you are now naturally, how you perform, how you behave - without thinking about it.

These are different stages that will last for varying periods of time and will replace each other or exist at times side by side.

You may go though some stages quickly, whilst others take more time.

Your ability to successfully see through any of these changes depends on your attitude towards them and how you think about them.

We understand these stages. Our role is to help you negotiate through each stage, providing support along the way.

CHAPTER 2

First things first

REDUNDANCY:
Know Your Rights – the Facts

A dismissal will only be a genuine redundancy if:

- Your Employer's business, or part of the business, has ceased to operate

- The business has moved to a different place

- The business no longer has a need for a particular type of work

Providing you have worked for your employer for a least a year, your employer must:

- Send you a written statement explaining why they are making you redundant

- And, hold a meeting with you to discuss the matter

- You have the right to appeal against your employer's decision

- It is unlawful to choose people for redundancy on the basis of their disability, sex, race, religion, sexuality or age, or because they are part-time or pregnant. In these circumstances, you may be able to claim compensation from an Employment Tribunal.

**By law you are entitled to redundancy pay.
The statutory rate is worked out as follows:**

- If you are under 22 you will be owed half a week's pay for each year you have worked

- This rises to one week's pay if you are aged 22 to 40, and one and a half if you are over 41.

Whilst every care is taken to ensure that the information provided in this guide is accurate, with changes in the law you should verify the facts before acting upon this information.

For more information Visit:

www.adviceguide.org.uk/index/life/employment/redundancy.htm

Preparation & Planning

"Never let a crisis go to waste" – Rahm Emanuel

(President Barack Obama's White House Chief of Staff)

Any expedition begins with careful preparation and planning – taking stock of what resources you will need on your journey and letting go of any baggage that will slow you down or hold you back.

For example, try to clear away any outstanding issues such as finalising your severance package as part of your compromise agreement **before** you leave your current employer. The longer your are on site the keener your employer will be to reach an agreement and see you off the premises.

Once you have agreed your severance arrangements it's a good idea to see an Independent Financial Advisor to provide advice on how best to handle your finances – which may include a lump sum severance payment - during your job search.

To find a Financial Advisor you could try the web site for The Financial Services Authority **www.fsa.gov.uk**

Consider carefully the temptation to take a holiday to get over the trauma of redundancy before you start your job search. You may return somewhat more relaxed and energetic but you will have lost valuable time in getting your job search underway. Consider negotiating a start date allowing you to go on a celebratory holiday once you have accepted a new job.

Plan to have the necessary requirements needed to allow you to undertake a concerted and focused job search eg:

- Office space at home – with no distractions!

- Computer with Internet access

- Ability to send and receive e-mails, faxes and texts

- A mobile phone

- Short term subscription with you local Newsagent to deliver relevant national, local and trade newspapers and magazines to identify advertised vacancies.

Points to consider:

If you haven't yet negotiated a finalised severance arrangement you may wish to request your employer to include provision for an Outplacement Consultant who can help you through the transition to a new life.

To find an Outplacement Consultant run a search on the Internet:

CHAPTER 3

List of source material

Some Useful Internet Sites

British Venture Capital Association
www.bvca.co.uk

The Directory of Management Consultants in the UK
www.mca.org.uk

The UK Directory of Executive Recruitment Consultants
www.askgrapevine.com

The International Directory of Executive Recruitment Consultants
www.askgrapevine.com

The European Directory of Non-Executive Director
& Interim Management Providers
www.askgrapevine.com

The European Directory of Career Management
& Training Consultants
www.askgrapevine.com

The Grapevine Index of Chairmen,
Chief Executives & Managing Directors
www.askgrapevine.com

The Grapevine Index of Human Resources Executives
www.askgrapevine.com

The Grapevine Index of Financial Executives
www.askgrapevine.com

The Head-hunter
www.headhunters.co.uk

The Society of Turnaround Practitioners (STP)
www.stp-uk.org

The British Franchise Association
www.franchiseworld.co.uk
www.franinfo.co.uk
www.whichfranchise.com
www.whatfranchisemagazine.co.uk
www.the-franchise-doctors.com

The British Coaching Academy
www.britishcoachingacademy.com

Times Online:-
100 Best Companies;
Top 100 Graduate Employers;
Top 50 Women; Senior Executive; Graduate
www.business.timesonline.co.uk

Kompass UK
www.kompass.co.uk

One Source
www.onesource.com

Hoovers (A Dun & Bradstreet Company)
www.hoovers.co.uk

Dun & Bradstreet – Key British Enterprises
www.dnb.com

Kellys Directory (60 day trial period)
www.kellysearch.co.uk

Local Businesses
www.indexlink.com

Business Start-up
www.uk-plc.net

Networking
www.businessdirectory-uk.co.uk

CHAPTER 4
Seven Steps to a New Life

Step 1 – Positioning for success

In most areas of life those who are consistently successful tend to share certain traits:

- They prepare to win
- They train – physically, mentally and emotionally
- They set goals and follow through unwaveringly
- They focus on their desired outcomes

In an interview situation, prospective employers anticipate interviewing a candidate with the following qualities:

- Confident, Self assured
- Relaxed, "comfortable to be with"
- Having a clear idea of what they want & where they are going
- Positive, forward looking
- Clear, fluent and articulate communicator

In short, someone who is operating at their peak level of performance. What prospective employers do not anticipate when interviewing a candidate are the following qualities:

- Tense, nervous, edgy
- Self deprecating, depressive, apologetic
- Aimless, not in control,
- Confused, rambling communicator

Employers report that the biggest turn off is a candidate who:

- Displays anger, resentment & bitterness towards his past employer
- Is stuck in the past

In short, they do not want someone with "baggage".

If you are stuck in the past and finding it difficult to let go of the painful emotions holding you back from moving on, you may wish to try an Emotional Release technique for releasing "negative" emotions so that the deeper, empowering emotions of self assurance and self confidence are freed to establish a robust, resilient emotional core upon which to move forward in life.

After a single session most people report that they feel relaxed, more energetic and have had insights into their lives which provide clarity of mind and a sense of purpose.

The technique is called SHEN Therapy and it involves putting the client into a state of deep relaxation whilst safely lifting troubling emotions to the surface to be released. The technique is not a "talk therapy" and is given almost completely in silence.

You may find it to be invaluable as a first step in your journey to a new life.

For more information and list of Practitioners in your area you may wish to visit their web site: **www.shentherapy.info** or **www.shentherapyuk.com**

Tip

Buy a copy of "The Secret" by Rhonda Byrne. ISBN No: 13:978-1-8473-7029-7. This remarkable book teaches the age old "Law of Attraction". It's a must accompaniment for your journey.

See the movie "YES man" starring Jim Carrey who plays a character who covenants to "Say Yes to everything....and anything" and transforms his life in amazing and unexpected ways. The film is very funny and uplifting with the underlying message that change and transformation can be as easy as just saying "Yes to Life!" The movie is based on the book by Danny Wallace.

SHEN Therapy Testimonials

"When we first met I had just been informed that I was about to lose my job. I was angry, scared, upset and generally "mixed up" and all I needed to do was find another job and life would be fine again. When you suggested that SHEN would be able to help me, to say that I was sceptical would be an understatement. However my wife, was very keen that I should do something as she had recognised a change in me that concerned her.

My first session was a revelation, I entered into it still sceptical but I had promised to go with an open mind, that session opened up a number of emotions that had been buried for over 30 years.

As you know I have now had a course of 10 sessions, feeling very confident and relaxed, I genuinely feel a great weight has been lifted off my shoulders. Am I still sceptical about whether SHEN works? No, I'm coming back for more!"

"I am pleased to recommend SHEN Therapy.
An engineering training meant that I was initially sceptical and cautious of the claims and theory of SHEN. It was therefore a very pleasant surprise to experience effects and benefits which I could not explain by conventional thinking. I believe that SHEN helped me through a difficult part of my life and restored some of the confidence I had lost.

I am immensely grateful for the care delivered during the sessions. The combination of this and the delightful surroundings of the centre meant I looked forward to each session and left the centre tranquil yet elated.

I hope that this affirmation proves useful to others and that they will avail themselves of the benefits of SHEN."

Step 2 - Options

"The quality of your life is determined by the choices you make"

You are now in the field of all possibilities. Use this time to consider all the options and ponder on the outcomes.

1. More of the Same

Most people opt for more of the same. A similar role in a corporate environment, preferably offering a bit more responsibility and an improved rewards package would do nicely.

Points to consider: To have a career with a future, it's a good idea to join a company with a future in an industry with a future – otherwise you may well find yourself back in the job market following "Outsourcing", Restructuring, Downsizing etc or an industry wide decline and technology transfer to a low cost country.

What's the alternative?

2. Interim Management

Interim Managers are increasingly used by Companies seeking to "bridge the gap" resulting from events such as someone taking a sabbatical, a lengthy recuperation from illness/accident etc, or to provide cover between one person leaving and another joining and so on.

Upsides:- Variety is the spice of life – different roles, challenges, environments, industries, locations etc. You do not get caught up in the internal politics, you have your independence, it can lead to offers of permanent work if you are interested and more importantly, it can be very lucrative.

Downsides:- When you are working its hard to be marketing and when you are marketing you tend not to be working. It can be a feast/famine where work is concerned with gaps between assignments. You may spend a lot of time travelling and away from home.

- **Market your resume to Interim Management Providers**
(You can download source material from www.how2surviveonline.com)

- **Develop your network of fellow Interim Managers.**

- **Set yourself up as a Limited Company**

3. Consultancy

Simply put: there are two main categories of Consultant:-

- The investigator/analyst

- The implementation/project manager/completer

Upsides:- Working as a Professional Management Consultant can be very rewarding – both financially and from a job satisfaction point of view.

You are usually awarded a high level of respect from your clients who are paying for your years of specialist knowledge and expertise. You can have the satisfaction of really "getting under the skin" of a client to identify significant opportunities for improvements and subsequent responsibility for implementation.

Management Consulting can provide you with the opportunity to quickly bring yourself up to date with best practice and can lead to offers to extend your assignment into a new brief and even to a full time position if you are interested. This allows you to find out all there is to know about a Company before committing yourself to a permanent position.

Once you have tasted the freedom to be your own boss you may never want to go back!

Downsides:- It can be a lonely existence with long periods away from home and at times isolated especially when the Management Team at the Client Company are concerned that your presence will lead to job losses and yet more re-organisation.

- **Set yourself up as a Limited Company**
- **Market yourself to Management Consultancy Practices**
(You can download source material from www.how2surviveonline.com)

4. Non Executive Directorships

Given the complexities and challenges facing businesses in today's global marketplace, it is no wonder that companies seek the advice of highly experienced individuals with a proven track record in business.

Upside:- Opportunity to use your life experiences and business acumen often in a mentoring and advisory capacity. It can pay very well (I know of one individual who has four non-executive Directorships which are his main source of income and drives a turbo charged Bentley!)

Typically you will attend around 10 meetings a year leaving plenty of time to pursue other activities.

17

Downsides:- Make sure you are aware of your legal responsibilities.

- **Develop your network of contacts for future NED appointments.**
- **Market your resume/CV to Non Executive Director Providers and ensure you are on their database.**
(You can download source material from www.how2surviveonline.com)

5. Venture Capitalists

Most Venture Capitalists are small bands of entrepreneurs who need to supplement their team with individuals possessing either specific or a blend of skill sets. These individuals will be used in a variety of ways e.g. as part of the Research Team identifying target companies, Investigative Consultants carrying out "audits" at short listed potential acquisitions, acting as an Interim Executive during the acquisition/possible acquisition/ restructuring/disposal phases.

Upsides:- Opportunity for building up equity holdings in single or multiple companies. Possibility of Buy In opportunities. Possibility of a permanent position.

6. Franchising

Always fancied the idea of running your own business but don't know where to start? Franchising provides an opportunity to develop a proven business model backed by the resources of a market leader in the field.

Upsides: Chance to be your own boss. Proven formula for success with documented history of people just like you who have realised their dream.

Downsides: Just as financial investments can go down as well as up, so even the seemingly most successfully established franchise can fail. Subscribe to Franchise magazines and check out websites.(See source material for website)

7. Charitable Work

From studying the outcomes of many 'Life Orientation' workshops, one area which consistently features is a desire to "put something back into Society", "help others", "be of service in some way" etc.

Use this programme to provide yourself with an opportunity for reflection on your life values which can lead to a new direction in life – one that will offer a challenge for your knowledge and expertise to make a 'real difference' to the lives of others whilst at the same time help in opening and ripening some of your own personal qualities such as compassion.

Working for a charity is not a 'soft option' and if you are involved in a front line operational role it can be at times a distressing and frustrating experience as well as a very fulfilling and rewarding one.

Voluntary Work

You may have decided to create a Life Plan that allows you time to combine both paid employment and voluntary charity work. Charities are always interested in receiving assistance from those with proven organisational and management skills.

Paid Work

With the requirement to respond on a global basis to urgent International Rescue missions such as earthquakes, tsunami's etc international charities are increasingly working together in groups such as 'DEC' to quickly raise huge amounts of money and materials and share logistics expertise to deliver aid etc where it is urgently needed – often in very inaccessible regions of the world. The list of specialist skills required is a long one and includes 'General', 'Operational', Management, Logistics, Finance, Human Resources etc.

Case Study

A recent Outplacement Candidate had been made redundant at the age of 60. Following his 'Life Orientation' workshop he identified a life style option offering him the opportunity to both utilise his considerable work experience and at the same time satisfy a life long interest in travel and a desire to 'put something back' into Society.

He chose to establish himself as an Interim Executive and to also offer his paid services to the major International Aid Agencies. The outcome was an initial – and very lucrative – six months Interim Executive assignment in China with an option to extend for a further six months; a request from a major Charity for help in the aftermath of the South Asia Tsunami, whilst at the same time assisting his family to establish a wildlife refuge and safari lodge in Africa.

8. Retirement

The most frequent comments I hear from recently retired Executives is "since leaving work I'm kept so busy I do not know how I ever found time to work".

There's often more to life than work. What usually stands in the way of our enjoying a better quality of life is FEAR. Fear of the unknown, fear of financial lack and so on. Active retirement can provide a very healthy antidote.

This could be your chance to do all those things you kept promising yourself such as joining a gym, playing golf or other exercise type activity to improve fitness; master the Internet and maybe become an ebay trader – very lucrative if you do it right; pursue a long cherished hobby; start a club or group or even a small business; go into property development, travel the world making new friends and experiencing new cultures; write a book; give talks to interest groups etc, etc. The list is endless, **AND** can generate extra income to supplement a pension or savings.

Step 3 - Life Orientation

Facing redundancy the natural reaction for most people is to want to start their job search **NOW!!**

But, it can pay great dividends to spend a little time in reflective preparation.

Have you ever wondered why it is that some people "always seem to land on their feet" are "born lucky" or seem to have the ability to "bounce back" no matter what the world throws at them?

From many years of interviewing a vast range of candidates, what has struck me most is how certain people always seem to be in the right place at the right time, taking advantage of every situation. Survivor not victim; not necessarily highly qualified, often not the most experienced candidate on a short list. They never the less seem to get selected and promoted over their peers. Why is this? The conclusion I've arrived at is that they are consciously or unconsciously following their true Life Orientation.

So, what is Life Orientation?

It's what comes naturally.

You are far more likely to succeed at something you feel passionate about or at least have a strong liking or interest for - something that comes naturally.

Life Orientation is all about finding out what's possible for you ...
and tapping into the opportunity to "follow your dream".

So, let's begin.

Step 1

Create a "personal road map". Place your intention in a bubble
in the centre of a blank piece of paper eg:- "My Future", "My
Career", "My Life" etc.

Step 2

From the bubble, draw out lines, like spiders legs. Now, on
each line place a word that describes what you are passionate/
interested in; what's important to you, what excites you; what
motivates you. Add likes, interests, hobbies, personal strengths,
qualifications etc; Add people you admire/respect whether alive
or historical.

Step 3

From each original line supporting one word add extra, adjoining
lines and on each one list a word/words expanding or describing
an aspect of the original thought. Keep words/phrases short,
simple, succinct.

Step 4

Look for synergies. Link the synergies using coloured pens. Let
the "personal road map" identify possibilities. Explore each one.

Step 5

Act on each one by setting priorities and time lines for their
achievements.

Good luck!

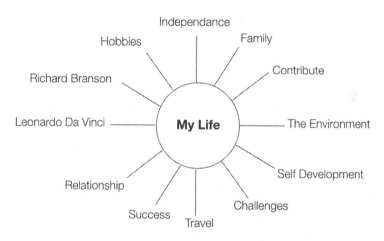

Step 4 -
How to design a winning CV

Because there is no standard format for a CV everyone has their own idea of how it should look. As anyone involved in recruitment will tell you, there are few things more tedious than reading several hundred CV's received in response to a recruitment assignment. Typically, your CV will be scanned by a Recruiter for a few seconds only.

So how do you ensure you do not fall at the first hurdle?

First, take time to consider format and content. Your CV is your "selling" document. First impressions count. So, here are some tips and examples to help you.

Curriculum Vitae (CV) is Latin for "course of life". Rarely, however, does a Recruiter or prospective Employer require or want a full biographical history. The ideal is to provide all the **pertinent** information presented in an attractive, easy to read, Resume format. See the following examples:

Resume/CV for applying for a Permanent Position:-

Page 1 – Split into 3 sections:-

Top Section details basic personal data including: Name and Address; Telephone, fax, mobile numbers; e-mail address, web site address if appropriate; date of birth (optional); status (optional); summary of education and qualifications.

Also to include a colour portrait photograph.

Middle Section to contain a 2 line "Profile" and a 2 line "Objective" statement.

The bottom Section to contain a career summary in reverse chronological order ie: most recent job at the top. Summary for each line to contain dates of employment, name of Employer and period of time/job title for each role held.

Designed in this way provides the person reviewing your CV/ Resume all the information required to make a selection from reading **one page only.**

Page 2 – Should comprise a description of recent employment history and achievements encompassing the previous 10 years (maximum) or the three most recent jobs held in reverse chronological order - ie: most recent job first.

Information should include:-

- Company name, location and brief description (number of employees, turnover, products, markets, production processes etc -- as appropriate) for current/most recent employer.
- Job title, reporting structure
- Key tasks in bullet point format. (Keep short & succinct)
- Achievements in bullet point format. (Keep short & succinct)

Repeat above for the preceding 2 jobs.

All of the above should ideally be on page 2 or if absolutely necessary running onto page 3.

Points to Consider:

- Never assume the Recruiter has heard of your current/ recent employer.
- Do not use acronyms or jargon.
- Keep it short, simple and succinct

- Think twice about writing your Resume/CV in a narrative format – the chances are it will not be read.

- Always ask for feedback on your Resume/CV but remember that everyone will have their own personal point of view. Do not be in a rush to make changes. Wait until you have a consensus of opinion before amending,

Hold your Resume/CV as a template on your computer. This allows you to personalise the content to be relevant to the position applied for.

Send as an email attachment, perhaps accompanied by a covering letter of application or introduction suitably personalised.

Incorporating a photograph in a Resume/CV is common in most other EU member states and North America. It is still rare to find a photo incorporated into a UK Candidate's Resume/CV. Include a digital, colour photo and you will stand out and be remembered.

I have seen CV's and Resumes with borders, printed on coloured paper in a wide variety of type faces and littered with icons. Take account of the profile of the Company to whom you are applying. You may win "brownie" points for submitting a highly original, eye catching Resume if applying for a creative role with an Advertising Agency but the same Resume may be considered outlandish and "over the top" if applying for a job in a Bank.

Resume/CV for applying for an Interim Management position
If you are considering a career as an Interim Manager then you will need to take a different approach to your Resume/CV to appeal to the specific requirements of the person reading it.

Remember, someone wanting an Interim Manager is more interested in your experience than employment history.
Prepare a 2 page Interim Manager Resume/CV.

Page 1: Split into 2 Sections:-

Top Section to include: Name & address; contact details ie: Telephone, Fax, Mobile numbers; email address; Web Site address – if appropriate; Nationality; Mobility; Summary of Education and Qualifications.

A two line "Profile"

Bottom Section to be split into 3 columns under the heading: Recent Assignments

Left column to be headed "Brief" or "Remit"

Middle column to be headed "Actions"

Right column to be headed "Outcomes"

Page 2 to be continuation of the lower part of page 1 in order to provide a good variety of assignments undertaken.

Include a section at the bottom of page 2 headed "Key describing words" listed in Sections ie:-

- Industry
- Products
- Markets
- Production Processes
- Job title
- Job function
- Knowledge/Qualifications
- Key areas of Expertise

Other than job title, try to use one word only to describe.

The key words will be used by Recruiters for searching data bases.

See sample Resumes for ideas and inspiration

(Sample Resume for Permanent position)
RESUMÉ

Name:	John Doe	
Address:	123 Any Road	
	Anywhere	
	UK	
	ABC 123	

Nationality:	British
Date of Birth:	(Optional)
Status:	(Optional)
Accommodation:	Houseowner – would relocate

Tel:	01111 2222
Mobile:	0222 11111

Education/ Qualifications:	FCCA BSc Computer Science with Software Engineering (Year 1)

Email:	johndoe@anyaddress.com

Profile: *An IT literate FCCA qualified Finance Director with multi-site responsibility for a global Group providing high-tech products, services and project based solutions to the International Energy Sector.*

Objective: *An influential Finance Executive role with a broadly based international business where the focus is on bottom line performance improvement.*

CAREER SUMMARY

03/2005 – to date	**ANY CO UK LTD** **Shared Services**		Finance Manager
09/2000 – 03/2005	PRIOR CO LTD Services Division	4½ yrs	Finance Director & Company Secretary
1995 – 09/2000	PREVIOUS CO LTD International Division	5 yrs	Finance Manager
1991 – 1995	EARLY CO LTD Overseas Division	2 yrs 2 yrs	Financial Accountant Budget & Systems Accountant
1987 – 1991	FIRST CO LTD Sales Division	2½ yrs 18 mths	Financial Accountant Budget Accountant

page 1

RECENT CAREER HISTORY & ACHIEVEMENTS

03/2005 – to date	:	**ANY CO UK Ltd –**
		Shared Services
Location	:	Anywhere
Business activity	:	The provision of shared finance, HR, facilities management and IT services across all UK operating Business Units. c12 Business Units employing c 2,800 employees
Position	:	**Finance Manager**
		Newly created position in newly established centralised shared services facility.
Reporting to	:	UK Finance Director
Supervising:	:	1 Assistant Accountant

Responsibilities
- On-time preparation and submission of monthly management accounts for the UK Shared Services Unit.
- Regular communication with the Shared Services Finance Controller based at Paris Headquarters.
- Allocation of all costs incurred on a fair basis to the various UK business units ensuring transparency.
- Providing Functional Heads of detailed analysis of costs incurred in support of their three year business plans.
- Ad-hoc exercises as required

Achievements
- Met all stringent deadlines set for reporting purposes
- Achieved a seamless transition from autonomous reporting by Business Units to centralised Shared Services.

09/2000 – 03/2005	:	**PRIOR CO Ltd –**
		Services Division
Location	:	Anywhere
No of employees	:	600
Business activity	:	Design, manufacture and installation of high value components supplied to major utilities, industrial companies and overseas customers. Company previously ABC Services Ltd until acquisition by PRIOR Co Ltd in January 2004.
Position	:	**4½ yrs Finance Director & Company Secretary**
Reporting to	:	Managing Director
Supervising:	:	(Initially) 9 comprising:
		o 2 Payroll
		o 2 Purchase Ledger
		o 1 Assistant Accountant
		o 1 Management Accountant
		o 2 Sales Ledger
		o 1 Cashier

Responsibilities
- Member of senior management team involving attendance at all monthly management meetings.
- Providing input into the formulation of strategic business plans
- Preparation, control and reporting of all budgets and forecasts
- Preparation and reporting of all monthly management and annual statutory accounts
- Attending weekly "Manufacturing Output Success" meetings
- Chairing weekly debtors' review meetings
- Project sponsor for SAP implementation
- Forming close working business relationships with the Business Finance Controller

Achievements
- SAP went live on time
- Gained Investors In People (IIP) accreditation
- Assisting in the move from Unit based accounting functions to a shared service approach entailing some involvement in reduction and redeployment of existing reportees resulting in a headcount reduction from 9 to 1.

Appointed Finance Manager of newly established central Shared Services facility

1995 – 2000	:	**PREVIOUS CO Ltd**
Location	:	Anywhere
No of employees	:	c400
Business activity	:	Design and manufacture of Super Products supplied to Utilities in the UK and overseas. Part of ABC Corporation Inc

Position	:	**5 yrs Finance Manager**
Reporting to	:	Managing Director
Supervising:	:	- 4: Payroll Clerk, Accounts Payable Clerk, Sales Ledger Clerk, Assistant Accountant

Responsibilities
- To safeguard the assets of the company
- To be the finance member of the Operations Management Team entailing attending monthly management meetings.
- Involvement in formulation of strategic business plans
- Ensuring accounts, budgets and forecasts were prepared and reported within timescales
- Supervising Accounts team responsible for: Payroll preparation; Sales Ledger; Supplier payments; VAT returns; Journal entries
- Involvement in the Group annual budget presentations at European headquarters.

Achievements
- Gained Investors In People (IIP) re-accreditation
- First Operations Management team role
- Gained a more comprehensive understanding of sales and operational planning
- Successful management of the accounts function during rundown to closure phase

(Sample Resume for an Interim/Consultant role)
INTERIM FINANCE DIRECTOR RESUMÉ

Name:	John Doe	Nationality:	British
Address:	123 Any Road	Date of Birth:	11.11.1111
	Anywhere		
	England		Mobile
	AB1 2CD		
		Education/	FCCA
Tel:	01111 2222	Qualifications:	BSc Computer
Mobile:	02222 1111		Science with
			Software Engineering
			(year 1)
Email:	johndoe@anyaddress.com		

Profile: *An IT literate, FCCA qualified Interim Finance Director with a strong record of delivering assignments and projects for high-tech businesses providing products, services and project based solutions.*

RECENT ASSIGNMENTS

Brief/Sector	Actions	Outcomes
Implement 'Shared Finance Services' function for a multi-site, multi-business Group.	• Allocation of all costs for various UK Business Units. • Ensuring transparency • Project implementation	Achieved seamless transition from Autonomous reporting by Units to Centralised Shared Services.
Implement SAP into large Manufacturing Business within the Energy Sector.	Project sponsor for SAP implementation.	SAP implemented on time.
Project manage introduction of Shared Services approach for diverse manufacturing/services provider to UK Utilities.	Transferred Business Unit based Finance to Shared Services approach.	• Headcount reduction • Redeployment • Gained IIP Accreditation
Various Finance Executive assignments.	• Member of senior management teams. • Formulating Business Plans • Budgets • Accounts preparation	• Achieved high profile recognition. • Project Leader • On time delivery • Cost reduction

Key Describing Words: *Interim, Consultant, Contractor, Finance, Accounting, Financial, Director, Manager, Executive, Company Secretary, Shared Services, Restructuring, Reorganisation, Multi-site, Multi-Business, Utilities, Energy, Manufacturing, Engineering, ACCA, FCCA.*

Step 5 - Marketing

The Internet

One of the most effective ways to learn of new job opportunities and ensure that your resume is despatched to interested parties - **WITH VACANCIES** - is to use the Internet.

A list of Internet job sites is attached but new ones are being added regularly.

Log on to the appropriate website using the website domain name on the list to follow.

You will most likely find that you have to follow a set procedure to register. Each site will vary in its requirements and format - but persevere - it will be worth it!

Some sites are linked so you may find your Resume/CV is automatically registered on other sites.

Use key describing words to assist in searching e.g.

Industry – Automotive, Electrical, Retail, Chemicals, Oil and Gas, etc

Markets – International, Distribution, Retail, B2B, Telecoms, IT etc

Products – Industrial, Consumer, FMCG, Toiletries, Components etc

Function – Finance, Sales and Marketing, Manufacturing, Engineering, IT, R&D, etc

Job-title – Sales Manager, Finance Director, MD, Chief Executive, IT Consultant, etc

Company Name – Subscribers to the job site may well be searching for someone from within their industry and will therefore often search by the name of a competitor, e.g. Ford, General Motors, Toyota, Asda, Littlewoods, Tesco etc.

Now sit back and await emails and 'phone calls!

Tip

Once you have added your details to the various job sites ask a willing employer to run an enquiry through the job providers site to ensure that your registration is identifiable for suitable positions (any willing employer will most probably need to have a password to run searches through the job providers' site).

We recently had a candidate whose details were not displayed following a search that should have brought up his identity. Upon investigation this turned out to be due to the fact that he had strung a number of words together to form a job title that was not recognised i.e. Technical/Development/R&D Manager. This was not picked up during the search. Once he entered a specific job title i.e. Technical Manager his identity came up immediately.

It may be necessary for you to make multiple listings.

List of Internet Job Sites

Top 10:-

www.exec2exec.com

www.exec-appointments.com

www.executivesontheweb.com

www.jobs.telegraph.co.uk

www.jobs.timesonline.co.uk

www.jobs.guardian.co.uk

www.goldjobs.com

www.allexecutivejobs.com

www.totaljobs.com

www.monster.com

Others:

www.hotonline.com

www.jobsite.co.uk

www.jobtrack.co.uk

www.jobsunlimited.co.uk (Guardian Jobs)

www.peoplebank.com

www.jobsserve.com

www.gisajob.com

www.topjobs.co.uk

www.cityjobs.com

www.jobpilot.com (International Jobs)

www.planetrecruit.com (IT, Telecom, Technology)

www.top-consultant.com (Consultants, Contractors)

www.top-execs.com

www.gaapweb.com (Accounting & Finance)

www.efinancialcareers.com (Finance & Banking)

www.careersforleaders.com (Public Sector)

www.personneltodayjobs.com (Human Resources)

www.peoplemanagement.co.uk

www.reed.co.uk

www.charitycareers.co.uk (Charities)

www.jobsincharities.co.uk (Charities)

Networking

What is Networking?

Networking is simply a compilation of anyone and **EVERYONE** you know that can be contacted to explore opportunities for employment. You can create a Net - it really does work! Some Outplacement Consultancies claim that 75% of all re-starts are the direct result of networking.

So, what do you do?

1. Go through your list of contacts and prioritise. Include current/ past bosses, subordinates, peers; suppliers; competitors; relatives; neighbours etc

2. Telephone the contact and say "I need your help and advice. I left/ am leaving .... and looking to move onwards and upwards. Can I send you my Resume/CV and contact you in a couple of days for your comments and suggestions."

It is best not to start asking questions about possible opportunities at this stage. It is better to wait until the contact has had the chance to review your Resume/CV and consider options.

3. When you ring back ask for feedback on your Resume/CV. Ask if your contact is aware of any opportunities for which you may be considered. If so make arrangements & follow up - and, good luck!

4. Do not hang up! Ask "would you be willing to give me the names and phone numbers of 2 people you know well enough for me to contact saying .... suggested I give you a call - I need your help and advice". Repeat step 2.

5. Repeat step 3.

Forget any natural "reserve", you may well be surprised at the amount of goodwill and willingness to help. They will all be thinking "there but for the Grace of God go I" ③⑤

There is a variation on networking.

Take a blank piece of paper.

On the left hand side list all the people you most admire:- family, friends, celebrities etc.

On the right hand side of the same page list all the things you most enjoy in life.

Look at the list. Look for synergy.

CASE HISTORY

- One candidate listed a very well know Entrepreneur as someone they admired.

- On the right hand side he had listed the things he most enjoyed in life.

- He wrote to the Chief Executive of one of the Entrepreneur's latest ventures enclosing his Resume and stating how much he admired the qualities of the said Entrepreneur, how they coincided with an area of his life he most enjoyed and how much he wanted to work in the new venture

- It got him an interview and a job.

NETWORKING IS VITAL!

If you haven't started your spreadsheet or list yet - **do it now!**

Networking Work Sheet (example)

Date	Name	Contact Number	Comments

The Role of the Executive Recruiter

There are various types of recruitment companies:-

High Street Employment Agency/Bureau

It is unlikely that these agencies will be handling the type of vacancy suitable for someone at Director/Executive/Manager level.

Profile

Most High Street Agencies operate on a contingency/success only basis. They obtain business by employers registering vacancies and by "canvassing on" vacancies by phoning around/mailing companies. Primarily their sphere of activity is in the recruitment of clerical, secretarial type appointments for permanent and temporary vacancies.

Recruitment Agencies

Again it is unlikely that Recruitment Agencies will handle the type of vacancies suitable for someone at Director/Executive/ Manager level.

Profile

Most Recruitment Agencies operate on a contingency/success only basis. Their sphere of activity is in the recruitment of specialist disciplines and lower supervisory and professional types of individual eg Service Engineers, Engineers (design, manufacturing, process etc), Assistant Accountants/ Accountancy personnel etc.

Executive Search & Selection Consultancies

These fall into 3 categories

1 Search
2 Selection
3 Search & Selection

1 Search

Search Consultancies almost invariably operate on an exclusive, retained basis. Many search consultancies claim to only employ search techniques ie: original desk based research. Some claim not to maintain a database and once an assignment is completed everything is filed/destroyed and candidate CV's are not retained.

Therefore if you are marketing your CV to Search companies you are relying on there being a suitable vacancy currently available which matches your qualifications and experience.

Plan to send copies of your CV to various named consultants over a period of time.

2 Selection

Most Selection companies will operate on an exclusive, retained basis. Selection consultancies tend to promote advertising as their preferred method of recruitment, so watch out for their adverts in the national, trade press and Internet sites.

Most will have a database although many are now rethinking the sense of this when they can access the database of the major Internet Service Providers.

They may have consultants who specialise by industry type or job disciplines eg: Electrical Engineering, Finance etc.

Generally, they will welcome receiving your CV and should acknowledge.

> If you have not heard anything for say 10 days or so, ring up and ask the receptionist to confirm that your details are registered on their database. If not, ask if you may forward a copy for his/her personal attention to ensure it is registered.
>
> Ask if there are specialist consultants. If so, ask to be put through to the one responsible for your discipline/industry etc. Ask for feedback on your CV, current state of the market for your discipline, offer to meet - DEVELOP A NETWORK - ring regularly.

3 Search & Selection

Search & Selection Consultancies normally work on an exclusive retained basis utilising search, selection and database file search techniques.

The same procedure can be followed as described above for selection.

Remember!

Recruitment Consultancies earn their living from fees paid by Client Companies and not candidates, so understand their possible reluctance to spend time speaking to you on the 'phone or meeting you in person. Their point of view may well be one of "my time is spent better with Clients on business development than engaging in speculative discussions or meetings with candidates".

What can you expect?

Acknowledgement. You should expect to receive some form of acknowledgement ie: e-mail, post, fax, or possibly, though unlikely - by 'phone.

If you want your CV to be read by a consultant - keep the covering letter brief and succinct.

Your Resume/CV can be "filed" in a number of ways:-

1. In its original form in a filing cabinet, alphabetically, or by discipline/industry etc - not very efficient!

2. Given attributes based on the contents of the Resume/CV. These attributes will then be "searched" for on the database eg Finance, Director, Electrical, Components, ACA etc.

3. Scanned into a computerised database.

4. Electronically transferred - if received by email - into a computerised database.

The trouble with methods 1, 2 & 3 is that your Resume/CV could be left lying around waiting to be read, coded, attributed, scanned into a database - or even lost!

Send your CV by email as an attachment.
Advantages:-

- Emails tend to be read on a regular basis

- Emails are usually acknowledged immediately

- Your CV is likely to be electronically transferred within minutes/hours of your sending it and therefore available for immediate consideration

Caution

A reputable Executive Search & Selection Consultancy will respect your confidentiality and will not reveal your identity to a prospective employer without your prior permission.

Alas! Not everyone is scrupulous. So, you might wish to add a confidentiality rider to your covering letter/ Resume/CV.

Direct Marketing to Prospective Employers

"There is never a shortage of Talent: There is only a shortage of great companies that the best people want to work for."

If you want a job with a future it helps to be in a profession, Company and Industry/Market Sector with a future.

"The world is: Mobile, Global, Temporary, Off-shored, Outsourced, Insourced, Upsized, Downsized and flooded with information – and will never be less so, for the rest of our lives."

Applying for jobs can be time consuming, frustrating, intensely competitive and, at times, quite demoralising as yet another reject letter saying the job went to someone better qualified, more relevantly experienced etc, thuds on your doormat.

The old Scouting adage " Be Prepared" is excellent advice. Here's what to do:

1. Firstly, determine your criteria ie: stay in same profession, same industry, same market, close to home etc, **OR** remove all barriers and be open to every possibility.

2. List your transferable skills

3. Do a SWOT analysis of your Strengths, Weaknesses, Opportunities and Threats.

4. Profile you ideals ie: Job Role, (full time, part time, permanent, temporary, employed, self employed, Executive, Board level etc), Company type eg: small, family run; medium, independent; multi-site plc group; International Corporation etc.

5. Research: Use the media (National, local, trade), Internet etc to identify companies meeting your criteria. Publications such as the Times publish lists eg: Times Top 100 PLC's; Top 100 Privately Owned Businesses; Top 100 Companies to work for; Who's Who in selected Markets etc

6. You might want to look into companies in your own vicinity

7. Do a SWOT analysis of those identified as Prospective Employers

8. Compare the Company SWOT analysis with the SWOT analysis of yourself

9. Look for synergies

10. Use the Internet to research your target companies in more detail

> **Tip**
>
> **Click onto the "Careers" page of their website. You may see your ideal job being advertised.**

11. Identify the level and name of your chosen level of contact eg: CEO, MD, HR Director etc

12. Prepare a personalised letter comparing your skill sets and values with those of the Company

13. Forward letter accompanied by your Resume, preferably by e-mail, to your chosen contact.

14. Follow up with a telephone call within 10 days

The beauty of this approach is that you may succeed in arousing an interest by one or more of your target companies who may invite you to what you may think is a speculative interview – where you are on a short list of **ONE** with everything to play for – only to find that they have a vacancy or they are willing to create one especially for you. **43**

Here is an example which used some of the above techniques to great effect.

A recent Outplacement Candidate had been made redundant from his job as Operations Director for a global business engaged in traditional manufacturing practices supplying long life, electro-mechanical products to the very established Public Utilities market.

He enjoyed his job as Operations Director but was concerned at the relevance of his professional qualifications, gained over a quarter of a century earlier and an ever shrinking UK manufacturing base and trend for outsourcing to low cost overseas countries. His solution was to move into the high technology sector.

He studied his transferable skills and did a SWOT analysis.

He reformatted his CV to emphasise his recent key job tasks, actions taken and outcomes, rather than a traditional employment history detailing past employers, thus overcoming possible reluctance by an employer to consider someone outside the high technology sector.

To gain credibility, he marketed himself to Interim Management Providers and obtained an Interim Role involving (a) completing a survey of the IT infrastructure of a large, centrally managed but Regionally based Company; (b) exploring the market place for "World Class" IT equipment and systems and (c) Roll out an Implementation/Replacement programme. This allowed him to market himself on a speculative basis to prospective employers in the High Technology market place which led directly to an offer as Operations Director for a global High Technology manufacturing Company.

"What is most valuable is what is most scarce. The scarcest resource in the quest to run a successful enterprise is TALENT!!"

Good luck!

Goal Setting

We take it as a "given" that any Executive will be familiar and practised in goal setting and understand its importance in measuring success.

Goal setting is VITAL to achieving your objective of a new career.

Step 1:- Identify your chosen routes to market eg:

- Advertised vacancies in National, local and trade media
- Internet job sites
- Intermediaries eg:
- Executive Search & Selection Consultancies
- Interim Management Providers
- Consultancies
- Franchisors
- Venture Capitalists
- Contact network etc.

Step 2:- Determine a minimum number of Resume mailings/ telephone contacts per day, per week.

Step 3:- Use a spreadsheet or manual record (see example on next page)

Activity Record (example)

Date	Company	Contact/Position	Tel No/Mobile	Email	Comments/Actions

Step 6 –

The Interview Process

Interview Preparation

STARTING POINT

Good News!

You've been invited to attend an interview with a prospective employer.

First Question: Is it worth attending the interview?

If the interview has been arranged by a Recruitment Consultancy ask them if they have the assignment on an exclusive or contingency basis. If it is exclusive, how many are on the shortlist? If you are say 1 of 3 or 4 the odds are much more in your favour than if you are being submitted on a contingency basis, in which case you may be 1 of 8-10 submitted by various recruiters. This may help you decide which interview to attend if there is a duplication of interview times/dates and a choice is necessary.

Use the Internet/local reference library to look up and download information from the company's web site or from an information provider eg: KOMPASS On-Line **www.Kompass.co.uk** or Dun & Bradstreet **www.dnb.co.uk** or Hoovers UK **www.hoovers.co.uk** (a D&B company)

Do you have a brief?

If you are being submitted by a Recruitment Consultancy then they should provide you with a detailed briefing document which includes:

- Profile of employer
- Organisation chart
- Job description
- Candidate specification
- Remuneration package

If they don't have a brief, it is unlikely that they have the assignment on an exclusive basis.

How to get there

Do you have travelling directions/map? **www.multimap.com** If possible reconnoitre ie: visit the location ahead of interview. This can prove invaluable in providing you with practical assistance in terms of:

(a) finding the place,

(b) finding a car park,

(c) locating the nearest train station, airport, bus stop etc.

You can observe the facility at your own leisure and form a view ie: does the place look well cared for or neglected and run down.

You may be able to ask questions of the locals eg shopkeeper, publican etc who will all tell you stories of expansion, redundancy, mergers etc and provide an insight as to the reputation the company has in the local community.

CONTINGENCY

Always have a contingency plan. What happens if you've decided to drive to the interview and your car won't start?

Don't Panic!

Place a list next to your phone which includes:-

- Name of interviewer/contact and direct/mobile telephone number

- Train & bus timetables - which would allow you alternative methods of travel in the event of breakdown, traffic jams, strikes or other natural disasters etc.

- The telephone number of the breakdown services and your ID or membership number.

- Name and telephone number of a relative/friend who would be available to take you. (This could save the day for someone with a leg in plaster for example).

GROOMING

Suit back from the cleaners? Shirt/blouse ironed? Boots blacked etc Dress appropriate to the interview or culture of the company. It can go against you just as much to be overdressed as "dressed down"

Protect yourself against the elements eg top coat, umbrella, etc

Interview Presentation Techniques

Timing

Always arrive early, say 15 minutes. Firstly, ask to use the washroom. Check out your appearance in the mirror - suit collar OK? Tie straight? Hair groomed? Shoes clean?

If needed to steady your nerves and "butterflies in the stomach feeling" try some deep breathing exercises. Breathe in through the nose whilst counting to 10, breathe out through the mouth whilst counting to 10. Try 5 - 10 sessions.

Finally look at your reflection in the mirror and smile. Take that "honest to goodness smile" out of the washroom with you.

Look around the reception area

This can be a mine of useful information. For example, look out for copies of the annual report and accounts, product literature etc but best of all, the company newsletter. This may tell you vital information eg the company has just won a major contract, is expanding, merging etc. It may also mention personnel movements.

For example the person interviewing you may just have been promoted from the role you are being interviewed for - hence the vacancy. So he/she will know all there is to know about the job - and see through anyone trying to pull the wool over their eyes.

Listen!

Listen to the receptionist/telephonist. Is the phone constantly ringing - with customers wanting to place orders - or creditors demanding payment. Listen out for company gossip!

Reception

How are you received? It is likely to reflect the culture of the company. Open, relaxed, friendly? Formal, efficient, professional? Surly - no eye contact - keep 'em waiting?

Do not smoke at any point in the interview process even if invited/offered.

Accept drinks eg tea, coffee if you wish, but never accept a biscuit. You are bound to be asked the most important question of the interview just as you bite into that crumbly delicacy and talking with your mouth full is not the best way to impress others.

Journey from Reception

Take in your surroundings. Are the offices/factory busy, lively, full of action? Are they full of the latest equipment, plant and machinery - in other words does the company look like a successful, profitable business investing in its future?

Inner Sanctum

Again, take in your surroundings as you enter. Is the room minimalist? Cluttered? Homely etc. In other words does it look lived in or is it only a short-lived home from home for a transient occupant.

How are you received? Are you expected? Is your Resume/CV open on the desk? Or lost in the mountain of clutter. Is the interviewer fully engaged with you or is he/she willing to accept endless interruptions and distractions.

Are you offered hospitality?

Are you put at ease with a warm and friendly approach or left to feel uncomfortable by a more formal, cool approach.

Are you called by your first name? Do you mind? How will you respond?

Does the Interviewer Explain the Process

Example:

- How long it will last?

- Who goes first?

- Will you be given an outline of the company and the role, if so, does this leave time for you to ask questions, talk about yourself etc.

Panel Interview

Oh dear! Fortunately not many companies still persist with panel interviews but you may have more than one interviewer present eg HR Director and the MD and/or Line Director/Manager.

Get the names and job titles of each panel member BEFORE the meeting!

Look at the person who asks the question but ensure that your reply is directed at/or includes your future boss if he/she is present - that's who you ultimately need to impress.

The Dynamics of the Selection Process

Usually the selection process consists of the employer trying to identify the ideal candidate, so the first part of the interview is usually spent with the company expecting the candidate to satisfy their requirements. So expect some tough questioning.

Sit in front of a mirror the night before the interview and rehearse the tough questions and watch your response eg:

"Why did you/do you want to leave your present job/last job?"

"Why should we offer you the job?"

Check out the library or try and get hold of a copy of a well known book "Great Answers to Tough Interview Questions".

The second stage is where the company believes they have found the man/woman of their dreams and try to convince you of the merits/benefits of joining the company. Sadly, many employers can be economical with the truth so beware! Do your homework and remember that they really want you, so do not be afraid to ask searching questions. It may well be your only chance.

Smile!

Remember to take that "honest to goodness" smile into the interview. A smile shows the interviewer that you are confident and relaxed and do not pose a threat. The instinctive reaction is to return a smile which leads to you feeling that the interviewer likes you and doesn't pose a threat. The result is RAPPORT!

Contacts

- Do you know who will be conducting the interview - name, job title etc

- Who else will be present?

- Is there a panel?

- How long has been allowed for the interview?

Support Materials

- Do you need any aids for the interview eg overhead projector, PC, flip chart, etc

- Do you need adapters etc for equipment

- Is your laptop/other equipment fully charged?

Step 7 - How to negotiate the package you want

Remuneration

You usually only get one chance to really negotiate the package you want, and that's at the offer stage.

The secret is to know how the system works and then work the system to give you what you want without appearing to make demands.

So, how do you do it?

First, ask if there is a grading structure. If for example the company has a grading structure from 1 - 10, 10 being MD and your job is grade 7 you have 2 further grades you can negotiate through.

Second, ask if the salary is on a scale for the grade: eg. let's say that the salary scale for a grade 7 is say £60,000 - £80,000 and they open with a figure of say, £62,500 then there is considerable scope for negotiation.

If you are offered a position where the grade is 9 and the salary offered is top of the scale, then no amount of negotiating is likely to result in an improved offer.

Third, ask when the salary is to be reviewed. It may be that you can bring the review date forward from say 12 months (anniversary) to say 3 months which means you can enjoy 9 months of the enhanced salary from the start of month 4.

Fourth, ask if there is profit sharing or bonus or both. How is it calculated - is it guaranteed, performance related, profit related etc. Is it percentage of salary?

How has the bonus paid out over the past couple of years - you may be surprised!

Are they prepared to guarantee all or part of the bonus for the first year?

Fifth, is there a "golden hello". This is a technique to get around the grading structure/salary scales issues without causing a revolt amongst the rest of the team.

Sixth - Benefits - Most important - notice period. Why?

Because if they wish to get rid of you it's better to be on a 12 month rolling contract than a 1 month fixed notice.

Most likely it will take you longer than 1 month to find another job which means you could be out of pocket.

It is unlikely to take you 12 months to find another job in which case you could bank a sizeable sum.

Company Car

- Is there a cash alternative?
- Is there a cash allowance?
- Is the car fully expensed?
- Can you get an upgrade?

Medical Insurance

- Is there medical insurance?
- Does it extend to spouse and family?
- Do you have to contribute? - How much?

Pension

- Is there a pension?
- How is it administered?
- Who makes what contributions?
- Is it non contributory on your part? (Result: more money in your bank account each month!)
- Is there an alternative whereby the company will pay into a personal scheme?

Relocation - What is included?

- Does the company have an arrangement whereby an agent will buy your home from you at market price allowing you to benefit from being a cash buyer?
- Will they re-imburse buying and selling costs eg estate agent fees, conveyancing costs, removal costs etc
- Will they contribute towards the cost of fixtures and fittings? i.e disturbance allowance.
- Will they provide temporary accommodation or an allowance for a period of time? How long?
- Will they pay for the family to visit the area and for compassionate visits home at weekends etc, during the house buying period.

And finally.......

Outplacement Provision

Life is fickle. The business world can be uncertain and turbulent. If you are going to be pushed out of an aeroplane it's a good idea to remember a parachute! No one likes to anticipate the worst, but an agreed outplacement package can ease the transition to a new future.

Just by asking some of the above questions, it may be possible to achieve a great remuneration package without appearing to be putting the company "over the barrel!"

GOOD LUCK!

References and medicals

One of the most frustrating aspects of job hunting is the time it takes. The process is often laborious and drawn out.

When you are told that you have a job "subject to satisfactory medical and references" you may think your worries are over. Well, "it ain't necessarily so".

Never assume – always prepare.

References

Ask close associates, previous bosses, subordinates, peer groups etc for (a) a written reference (it's very hard for them to go back on their printed word) and (b) their willingness to give a verbal reference if approached. Do not assume they are in possession of all the relevant facts and information or even that they will give you a good reference.

If in doubt – leave them out.

Ensure that they are willing and ready. Provide them with a copy of your Resume as the prospective employer may quote from it or provide the relevant dates, facts, responsibilities, achievements etc.

Above all **ASK** if they are comfortable about giving you a positive reference.

Medicals

Usually, most companies require only a superficial medical which is often provided by a request to visit you own GP or attend the Company Doctor.

You could pre-empt this by paying for a private medical with your GP who will provide you with a report declaring your fitness for work. This may well be enough for some employers or may convince them sufficiently to confirm the offer and arrange a start date.

Start date

Having confirmed in writing your acceptance of the offer the last detail is to confirm start date.

General Advice - The sooner the better!

Points to Ponder

- Have you pre-booked holidays arranged - can you alter the dates - do you want to, does the company want you to. Do not get off on the wrong foot by failing to mention pre-booked holidays until after you start. It may interfere with a planned induction programme or important meeting/conference etc.

- You may wish to take some holiday before you start - so that you (a) will have a clear run without interruptions for the first important months in the job and (b) you will hopefully feel fit and relaxed and eager to start.

- You may need some time to sort out accommodation and organise relocation. You will definitely score "brownie" points with your spouse/partner if you are there to help sort everything out rather than leave it all to your 'other half' to organise everything whilst you are working round the clock trying to familiarise yourself with your new job and make an impact. The company is also likely to appreciate your total commitment to the job in hand without interruptions involving house hunting etc.

Sample Letter 1 – Response to Advertised position

Name
Address

Tel   :
Mobile   :
Email   :

Date

Private & Confidential
Name
Title
Department
Address
Address
Post Code

Dear

Re: **(Position) advertised in (media) on (date)**

I read with great interest details of the above position and enclose a copy of my Resume for your consideration.

Business Profile:

Key Areas of Expertise:
- *List*

Personal Characteristics:
- *List*

I should welcome the opportunity to discuss my background in greater detail and look forward to hearing from you.

Yours sincerely/faithfully

Enc

Sample Letter 2 – Speculative letter to Executive Search & Selection Companies

Name
Address

Tel :
Mobile :
Email :

Date

Private & Confidential
Name
Title
Department
Address
Address
Post Code

Dear

Re: Current Recruitment Assignments

I am pleased to enclose my Resume for your
consideration for assignments you are currently handling.

Please feel free to circulate my Resume amongst your fellow
consultants and hold my details on file.

I look forward to hearing from you and would welcome an opportunity
to meet you at a convenient time and date.

Yours sincerely

Name
Enc

Sample Letter 3 – Speculative approach to Prospective Employers

Name
Address

Tel   :
Mobile :
Email :

Date

Private & Confidential
Name
Title
Department
Address
Address
Post Code

Dear

Re: Opportunities with (Prospective Company Name)

I am pleased to enclose my Resume for your consideration for
possible vacancies within your company.

Business Profile
Key Areas of Expertise
(List)
Personal Characteristics
(List)

Please feel free to circulate my Resume amongst your colleagues
and hold my details on file.

I look forward to hearing from you and would welcome an opportunity
to meet you at a convenient time and date.

Yours sincerely

Name
Enc

Sample Letter 4 – Speculative approach to Interim Management Providers

Name
Address

Tel   :
Mobile   :
Email   :

Date

Private & Confidential
Name
Title
Department
Address
Address
Post Code

Dear

Re: **Interim Management Opportunities**

I am pleased to enclose a copy of my Resume for your consideration for current and future Interim Management assignments. Please feel free to circulate my details amongst your colleagues and include on your database.

Business Profile

Key areas of expertise
list

Key describing words:
list

I should be pleased to introduce myself personally to discuss how I could contribute to your clients.

I look forward to hearing from you.

Yours sincerely/faithfully
Enc

Resources for Interim Managers

Books

Interim Management – by Dennis Russell
Hardcover – 200 pages @ £26.99
Published 1998 Butterworth-Heinemann, ISBN: 0750639776

Business Guide to Interim Management

Published by Caspian Publishing in association with Ashton
Penney and the CBI.
Available from a link on the Ashton Penney website
(**www.ashtonpenney.com**) - £15

Company Formation/Management

Orchard House, Park Lane, Reigate, Surrey RH2 8JX
Tel: 01737 244 682 **www.competex.co.uk**

Giant Group
Angel House, 338-346 Goswell Road, London EC1V 7LQ
Tel: 020 7520 0500 **www.giantgroup.co.uk**

Professional Indemnity & other services:

Jardine Freelance Services
PO Box 172, Woking, Surrey GU21 5YS. Tel: 01483 251 146

T L Dallas (City) Ltd
Ibex House, 42-47 Minories, London EC3N 1DY. Tel: 020 7816 0210

Industry Associations:

Institute of Interim Management, Management House, Cottingham
Road, Corby, Northants, NN17 1TT. Tel: 01536 207 307
www.ioim.org.uk

Interim Management Association,
36-38 Mortimer Street, London W1N 7RB Tel: 020 7462 3296
www.interimmanagement.uk.com

NOTES